SAI
THOMAS

Christopher Harper-Bill

Scala Publishers Ltd
and Cathedral Enterprises Ltd

THOMAS BECKET is the best known of all English saints. Although a Londoner by birth, he will always be associated primarily with the Cathedral Church of Canterbury. He served as archdeacon of the diocese before he became archbishop. He staunchly defended the privileges of his office and his church, and in 1170 he returned to England to face martyrdom in the Cathedral for them. Within a few years the cult of the murdered archbishop raised Canterbury to the status of a major centre of western European pilgrimage, while his example was an inspiration to all.

The story of the relationship between Archbishop Thomas Becket and his earthly lord, King Henry II, has a perennial fascination because it involved the clash of two powerful personalities. Their conflict, however, has a more fundamental significance. It was one particularly dramatic episode in the long struggle, lasting from the late 11th century to the early 14th century, between a universal church under papal leadership and the feudal monarchies which were to develop into the nation-states of Europe. The rulers of these kingdoms had at their disposal not only brute force but also an increasingly sophisticated bureaucratic machinery, and the career of Thomas Becket, before his elevation to the archbishopric, is itself an illustration of the growing professionalism of royal government in the 12th century.

ABOVE *An apparition of St Thomas from his shrine. In early 13th-century glass, one of the 'Miracle Windows' at Canterbury Cathedral, St Thomas issues from a shrine. This image is unusual in depicting a raised shrine, rather than the tomb in the crypt where many of the miracles were said to have happened.*

RIGHT *The site of St Thomas's martyrdom is in the north-west transept of Canterbury Cathedral. The altar, known as the 'altar of the sword's point', with the bronze sculpture representing the cross and two swords above it, was given this new form in 1986.*

THOMAS

Born in London in 1118 of Norman parents, Thomas Becket was educated at Merton Priory and at a city grammar school. His passport to fortune was entry into the household of Theobald, Archbishop of Canterbury, in 1139. He studied both law and theology in continental Europe, but he was no scholar and merely did enough to make his way as a top administrator. He was appointed archdeacon of Canterbury in 1154, and early the next year the archbishop commended him to the newly crowned young King Henry as his chancellor.

Becket turned this position of head of the royal writing office into something new. He was no mere senior secretary, but became the formulator and executor of government policy. He proved himself a staunch advocate of monarchical control over the Church, rejecting papal interference. He planned a great, if ultimately abortive, expedition in 1159 to vindicate Henry II's claim to Toulouse. The magniaficence of his embassy to the French king was widely remarked. He was a worthy and proud servant of one of the most powerful rulers of the western world. His celibacy and continence were hardly any indication of the dramatic change to come.

In May 1162 Henry obtained the appointment of Becket to the vacant archbishopric of Canterbury, intimidating monks and bishops into acceptance. Becket desperately attempted to dissuade the king, realising that Henry's vision of close cooperation was a mirage. Once he sat in the chair of St Augustine his loyalties must lie not primarily with the king, but with God, the universal Church and his own see. His change of heart and mind was signalled by his resignation, to Henry's fury, of the chancellorship.

The conflict which developed over the next few years can be understood only in the context of the papal reform movement initiated in the late 11th century, and associated primarily with Pope Gregory VII (1073–85). This reform was not confined to the Church in the narrow sense but affected the whole Christian community, for the pope had decided that the root cause of all evil within society was lay domination of the clergy at all levels and, above all, the tyranny exercised over the Church by kings. The Church must have freedom to fulfil its divine mission. Secular monarchs, who had for centuries enjoyed the status of God's deputies on earth, were suddenly demoted to being mere agents of papal and priestly authority. A king was inferior to any minister of the church, for priests had to answer to God even for the souls of princes. Western European rulers lost the intellectual argument but they did not, of course, abandon the struggle. They attempted to regain control of the Church through new administrative techniques, through intimidation and through their extensive patronage. In practice a balance of power emerged in the 12th century in most kingdoms, but Becket determinedly adhered to the full programme of Gregory VII.

It was unfortunate for Becket, as a defender of ecclesiastical liberties, that the then pope, Alexander III (1159–81), was engaged in a difficult struggle against the German emperor Frederick Barbarossa (1152–90), who was seeking to subdue northern Italy and supported a rival pope. Alexander III spent much of the 1160s in exile, first at Sens and then at Benevento, and he simply dared not drive Henry II into the imperial camp by unreserved support for Becket.

Becket's first months as archbishop were characterized by a series of petty disputes, a clear indication that he meant to claim for the Church the entirety of that ambiguous borderland between royal and ecclesiastical jurisdiction. Matters came to a head in October 1163 when Henry II, as part of his great drive against all forms of criminality in England, proposed to the bishops that clergy convicted of misdemeanours and felonies in church courts should be handed over immediately to the secular arm for salutary and

BELOW *Effigy of Henry II: Henry was buried in the abbey church of Fontevraud (Maine-et-Loire); beside him are his wife Eleanor of Aquitaine and his son Richard I. Fontevraud was a nunnery in the heartland of Henry's continental dominions and was one of his most favoured religious communities.*

LEFT *Seal of Thomas Becket: this was the Archbishop's personal seal. It may seem odd that it was made from an antique gem engraved with the figure of a Roman god or hero, but such antique gems enjoyed enormous prestige in the early Middle Ages.*

RIGHT *The 'Waterworks' Plan, a double page from the Eadwine Psalter showing the plumbing system installed by Prior Wibert (1152–67). This is a unique surviving image of Canterbury Cathedral as it was in Becket's time, before the fire of 1174 that destroyed its east end. Becket's own palace is not shown, but was situated to the top right of the church on the plan.*

BELOW *Charter granted by Thomas Becket as Archbishop of Canterbury, one of the very few surviving charters from his time of office.*

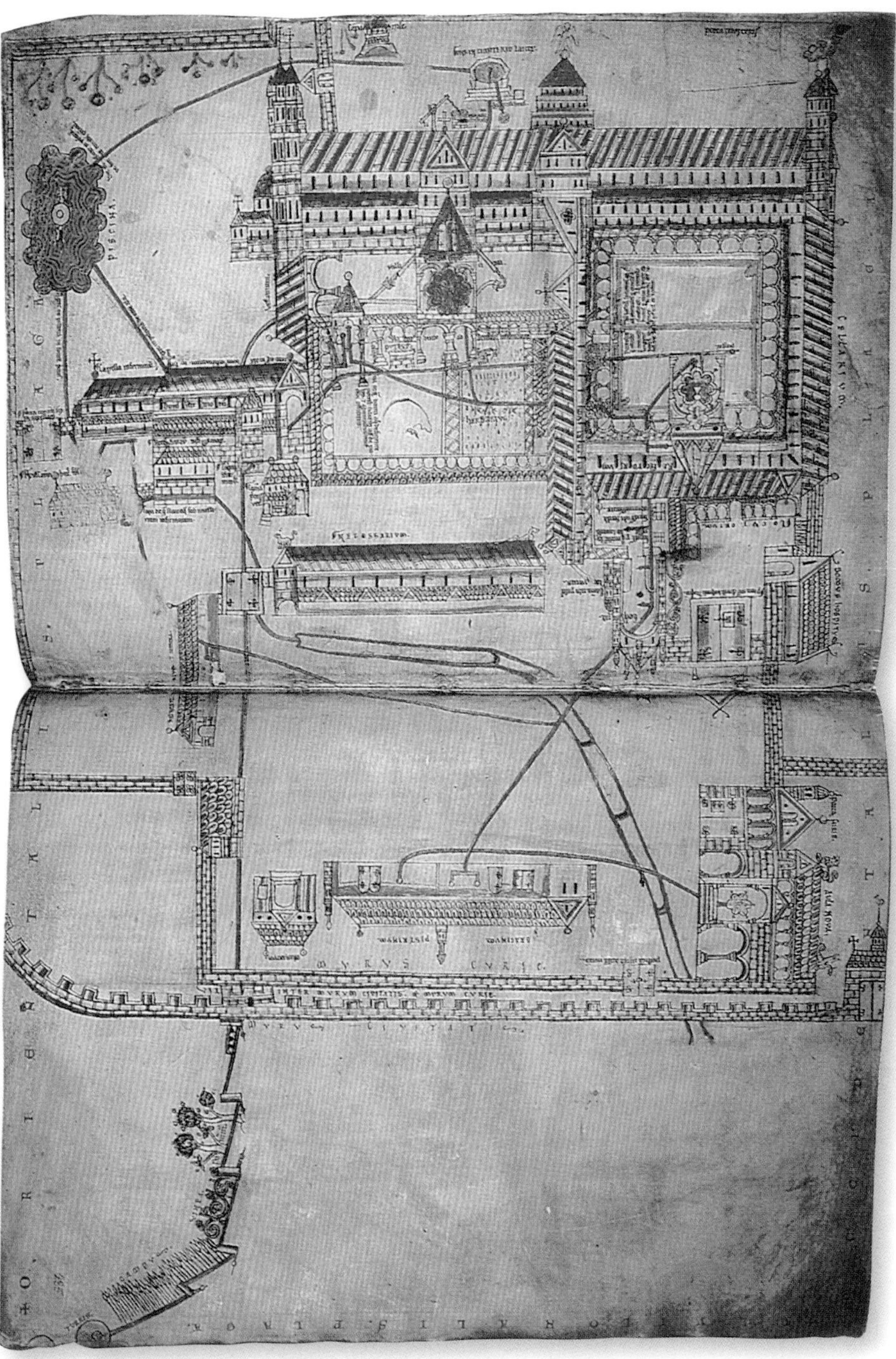
PISCINA
capella infirmorum
CELLARIUM
aula nova
MURUS CURIE
INTER MURUM CIVITATIS & MURUM CURIE
MURUS CIVITATIS

exemplary punishment. The king's stance is understandable, for clergy or 'clerks' included not only parish priests and monks, but married men who had received the first tonsure, perhaps as many as one in six of the adult male population. Becket, however, asserted that 'God does not judge twice for the same offence', and that degraded clerks should be answerable to the royal courts only for another crime subsequently committed. The canon law of the Church, which was only beginning to be formulated at this time, was ambiguous on this point. Becket, however, was determined to defend the complete autonomy of ecclesiastical jurisdiction. For him, the clergy should have no other king than Christ and should be subject to His law.

Faced by this resistance, Henry II broadened the issues at stake, and at a council at his palace of Clarendon in Wiltshire in January 1164 demanded that the bishops should accept sixteen 'constitutions' which set out the relationship between Church and Crown in England as it had been in the time of his grandfather Henry I (1100–35). The Constitutions of Clarendon not only restated the royal view on criminous clerks. They also stipulated that cases about ecclesiastical patronage should be heard in the king's court; that no baron might be excommunicated, nor might any bishop leave the realm nor any appeal go to Rome without royal consent; and that episcopal elections should in effect be controlled by the king. All this had been the situation in Henry I's time, but in the interim the English Church had achieved greater freedom and not even the many royalist bishops felt that they could consent to such a scheme when set down in writing. Then, suddenly, Becket capitulated under pressure and agreed to Henry's demands. He soon repented bitterly and withdrew his consent, but this moment of weakness was disastrous, for it convinced most bishops that the former chancellor, whom they had never wanted as archbishop, could not be relied upon.

Henry was now determined to break his former friend, believing Becket to have betrayed him unforgivably. Becket was cited to appear before the king's court as lord of Canterbury, in a matter which was clearly feudal and temporal rather than spiritual. He failed to respond and was hence guilty of contempt of court. He was charged with this at the Council of Northampton in October 1164, when the king also accused him of financial dishonesty during his time as chancellor. Henry's behaviour at the council does him no credit. He harangued the bishops and cajoled the

RIGHT *Becket's story in* The Becket Leaves, *a four-leaf fragment which is all that survives from a 13th-century verse* Life of St Thomas Becket. *On the left of the image, Henry expels Becket's friends and kinsfolk. After the archbishop withdrew into exile in 1164, the king conducted a campaign of attrition against all associated with him. On the right, Becket lies sick through excessive fasting while at Pontigny. His austerity and asceticism from the time he became archbishop were an attempt to atone for his past life and to make a new beginning.*

Par le roi est exillez
De thomas tut li parentez
Hors de terre nest esparni
Ne li iouenes ne li chanu
Ne la femme ken gisine
Tient sun enfant a sa peitrine
Ne mangue fors du pulment
Dunt serui fu li cuuent
Viandes artes sanz savur
Veille de nuit, iure de iur
Mais co li est de suffrir grief
Tendre fu nurri e suef
Tant se met en grant destresce
Kil par tant tens sun cors blesce
Travailz kil out avant duble
Mais lestat de sun cors truble
Ne puet li cors sustenir
Ke li quers out en desir
Pa ieune adle quor fade
Cuchez sen est par tant malade
Un suen seint confessur
Ki mult lama par grant tendrur

Cumande par obedience
Kil vive atempreement cumence
Cuis ne volt estre a cuntraire
Mais ses cunseilz e cumandz faire
Si nun la vie eust perdue
Sa manere change e mue
Si sei amesure ne fust
De feblesce mort geust
Mais deus lad par sa vertu
La vie e sante rendu
Henris li rois dengleterre
Tant est irez ne set ke fere
Treistre voit de iur en iur
Sun repruvier e deshonur
Mult est laidiz e escharniz
E maudit co peise li
A lapostoile enveit a dire
Ke trop dure enterenz celuire
Lacord mult desire e veit
Ke ele nest faite mult sen deut
Messagers vienent e vunt
Ki alez e repairez sunt

Par ses ieunes e uraisuns
Veilles e afflictiuns
Febles est le quor ad fade
Cuchez sen est malade
Par force de obedience
Amenda puis cele abstinence
E li apostoille respunt
Ki le desturbe peche funt
Mais ne feroient legerement
Pes fors par commun asent
Sil fussent andui present
Pais feroient a tel parlement
Si ensemble eussent parle
Tost enseroient acorde
Mais li rois ni asent pas
Kensemble soient il e thomas
Li arceuesques a co respunt
Ne place a deu ki fist le mund
E pur nus mort suffri en croiz
Ke en i eusse la tierce voiz
Kar la pape par faus treire
Purroit faus iugement feire

PREVIOUS PAGE *Henry II and Archbishop Becket arguing, as represented in the 13th-century style stained glass in the Trinity Chapel. The scene is probably the Council of Northampton, which took place in October 1164. Henry accused Becket of contempt of the royal court, and of embezzlement while he had been chancellor. Becket stormed out of the council, though not all agreed with him. The Bishop of London remarked, 'He always was a fool, and always will be'. A few days later he went into exile.*

BELOW *Pontigny, a Cistercian abbey near Auxerre in France, where Thomas spent the first two years of his exile. He left the abbey in November 1166 after King Henry had threatened to confiscate all Cistercian property in England in retaliation. St Edmund of Abingdon, another canonised Archbishop of Canterbury (1233-40), is buried here. The building as it stands today is in the early Gothic style (late 12th century).*

barons in order to obtain the verdict on which he was intent. Before it could be delivered, however, Becket stormed out of the council. In disguise he took a circuitous route to the Channel coast, making ultimately for Sens and Pope Alexander, to whom he had already appealed.

The archbishop was to remain in northern France for the next six years, first at the Cistercian abbey of Pontigny and then at Sens. There were constant diplomatic efforts to resolve the dispute, but while the issues at stake dominated Becket's and his circle's whole lives, for Henry II there were many other problems to be resolved in every province of his extensive empire, in none of which did the Archbishop of Canterbury find an imitator.

LEFT *Vézelay in Burgundy, where Becket excommunicated his adversaries in 1166. One of the foremost examples of French Romanesque architecture, it was the centre of the cult of St Mary Magdalene and was rebuilt between 1120 and 1150 on the proceeds of pilgrimage.*

ABOVE *Scenes from* The Becket Leaves*: On the left, St Thomas excommunicates those accused of crimes and outrages. These sentences, delivered at Vézelay on Whit Sunday 1166, were directed not only against the king's agents but against the Bishop of Salisbury, a former supporter who had capitulated to strong royal pressure. Positions had hardened to a point where reconciliation seemed impossible. On the right, the Council of Montmirail, January 1169, convened mainly to settle political differences between Henry II and Louis VII of France, but also attended by papal legates. King Louis had protected Becket for over four years, but now became impatient with his apparent intransigence.*

The pope, who returned to Italy in November 1165, supported Becket in principle but seems to have despaired of his intransigence, which threatened to provoke the equally obstinate king into severing relations with the legitimate papacy just at the time when the independence of the Roman Church itself was under threat from a determined emperor.

Henry was uncharacteristically vindictive in his harassment of the archbishop's kindred, friends and clerks, but Thomas responded in kind by excommunicating the king's main agents at Vézelay on Whit Sunday 1166. The bitterness of feeling is revealed by the exchange of vitriolic letters in that year between Becket and Gilbert Foliot, Bishop of London, a reforming prelate himself but one who believed that the welfare of the Church was best achieved by cooperation with the Crown. There were appeals and counter-appeals to the pope, who despatched a succession of legates to resolve the dispute, but without any success. By 1169 a settlement seemed no nearer. At a conference at Montmirail in January Becket, by his refusal to accommodate, brought despair even to his protector, King Louis VII of France. In April he excommunicated Gilbert Foliot, his

RIGHT *The parting of Becket and Pope Alexander III, as shown in* The Becket Leaves. *One of the great legislators of the medieval Church, Alexander was himself in exile from Rome, at Sens, from 1162 to 1165. He supported Becket in principle but was justifiably terrified that, if he took up Becket's cause too energetically, Henry II would transfer his support from Alexander to the Emperor Frederick I, leaving the pope in a very weak position.*

ɜ solat. 7 stare admonet in causa assumpta viriliter

Quant pes fu a honur mise
Entre lempire e seinte iglise
La pape de france sen part
Ki mut pe(n)se ke deus la gart
Larceuesq; lad cunuie
Desq; en burges la cite
La sentre[illegible] e sen returne
Lun e lautre sen par murne
La pape va uers Rume droit
E larceuesq; benoit
Apres cele departie
Ne le uit unc en ceste uie
Larceuesq; ki a puntenui
Repaire u sent tapi
E meine solitaire uie
En estr[illegible] e estudie
En ieune e en uraisun
Ueille e contemplaciun
[illegible]

Li enuius e li engres
Ki tost destuba cele pes
[illegible]uie ke puet deuenir
Ke ne set sa pes tenir
Au tirant henri mult peise
Ke larceuesq; est tant a eise
Ki sen ur ke nuls la uue
Diluec cuuent kil le remue
Au chapistre de cisteaus
Mande kil ne li sunt leaus
Ki sun mortel enemi
Funt tel solaz e tel abri
Cist ki mun enemi acoit
A moi honur ne bienue uoit
Ki mun enemi auance
A moi fait mal e desturbance
Sil nel facent amender
Mult lur toudra grant auer
De lur granges e maisuns

LEFT *A stone relief showing St Thomas Becket, set into the wall of Sens Cathedral. It is reputed to have been made originally in the late 12th century for a private house in Sens.*

RIGHT *Sens Cathedral, one of the earliest large churches to be completed in the new Gothic style, which originated in the area around Paris. Becket was in exile here from 1166-70, just at the time when the new cathedral was being completed. It was no coincidence that the Sens master mason, William of Sens, commenced the new design of the eastern part of Canterbury Cathedral after the great fire of 1174.*

ABOVE *St Thomas leaving Montmirail, as shown in* The Becket Leaves. *He is reproached by the two kings, Henry and Louis, and their followers, but the poor folk seek his blessing. He returned to Sens, where on Palm Sunday 1169 he excommunicated his great ecclesiastical rival, the Bishop of London.*

Coronat' rex h. iunior p manu rogi archiepi ebor' i p iudiciu ecce cant. Celebrat' conuiuiu coronatois r

En pes se tient e patience
Ne remaudit. Grundist ne tence
Un de ses clers li dist beu sire
Eu murs kad nun martire
Fu traite hue de timeorde
Ke a la verite se acorde
Kar par martire ert taine
Bien le uus devin finie
Par une mort seinte iglise
Conquerra pes e franchise
Larceuesq; a co respunt
Co pleise a deu ki fist le mund
Pur sa tre seurer
Et tut sun regne cousiner
Sun fiz hert eir a Westmust'
Henri li reis ueut coruner
D[illegible] plusurs tut [illegible] greuer
[illegible]endre e entamer
L[illegible] e la franchise
A larceuesq; e sa iglise
Grant gent i estoit banie
De clerge e de chevalerie

Li reis henris grante e dune
De engleterre la curune
A sun fiz esne henri
Repentant fu puis e marri
Li prelat deuerwic roger
A tort lempruist a curuner
Roger deuerwic i fu
Li arceuesques cuneu
Leuesq; fu de lundres la
Eist de [illegible]cestre i ua
Li euesq; [illegible] Salesbire
Cuntre lotrii de cantrebire
Oue larceuesq; cist tut troi
Furent a coruner le roi
Henri le iofne las liure
Mut en auint mesauenture
La feste fut pleuerement
Du mang' eurent grant gent
Le pere fist au fiz grant feste
Ne oimes en chantun neu geste
Ki fust de riche hom seruu
Cum fu li iofne reis henri.

Li peres li fist ioie
Ka ceu iur li fu s[...]
Oiant plusurs g[...]
Ke sul fu reis iofu[...]
Ne mie cist ki din[...]
Dunt mut apres [...]
Mut sen dolut en a[...]
Kar poi dura lam[...]
Apres poi dure sei[...]
Kil au pere guerr[...]
Co fu au cumenc[...]
Le p̄mer encuch[...]
Du peche lu roi [...]
Ki seint thomas [...]
Quant li plat de [...]
Loi recunter e [...]
Mut se tint desp[...]
E mut sun hom[...]
La dignete de sa [...]
Mut desuncunbre[...]
Asez les enfis cha[...]
E par la pape am[...]

greatest ecclesiastical rival, who responded by claiming that London rather than Canterbury should be the archiepiscopal see. By the summer Henry II feared a papal interdict on his lands, yet even now, at a meeting at Montmartre in October, the king refused to give the kiss of peace on which Becket insisted if there was to be a reconciliation.

Becket's return to England was prompted by an event unrelated to the main conflict. On 14th June 1170 Henry, in order to secure the succession, had his eldest son, Henry, crowned by the Archbishop of York. This was a violation of the traditional right of the church of Canterbury, and marked a new phase in the rivalry of the two archbishops which had persisted since the Norman Conquest. Henry, once more afraid of ecclesiastical sanctions, met Thomas at Fréteval in July. He accepted Canterbury's position on the issue of the coronation, but there was no discussion of the Constitutions of Clarendon. Both parties felt that they had gained the day, which was hardly a solution. In fact, the archbishop was now determined to return in order to protect the privileges of his own church. Landing at Sandwich on 1st December, he was met by the intransigent hostility of a gang of king's men, but also by the adulation of the common people. His entry into Canterbury, as recounted by his biographers, had marked parallels with Christ's entry into Jerusalem on Palm Sunday.

LEFT *The coronation of the young King Henry, eldest son of Henry II, on 14th June 1170, as shown in* The Becket Leaves. *It was conducted by the Archbishop of York, assisted by the Bishops of London and Salisbury. On the right the two kings, father and son, are shown feasting. The heir to the French throne was often crowned during his father's lifetime, but this was a novelty in England.*

Becket refused to absolve the Archbishop of York and the Bishops of London and Salisbury from the papal sentence of excommunication for their participation in the coronation, and himself excommunicated those who had despoiled and still retained the archiepiscopal estates. These actions prompted complaints to the king, still in Normandy. Henry had already been discussing with his councillors how the archbishop might be restrained – house arrest was certainly envisaged – but his famous outburst, which provoked four prominent knights of his household to set out to kill Becket, was almost certainly unpremeditated. The words of the outburst are variously given, most authoritatively as: 'What miserable drones and traitors have I nourished and prompted in my household, who let their lord be treated with such shameful contempt by a low-born clerk'.

Equally surely, Thomas had not been courting martyrdom when he returned to England but intended rather, by a firm course of action, to vindicate the rights of his see and of the Church against assaults both from the king and from petty predators. Yet when the four knights arrived at Canterbury on the evening of 29th December 1170 and confronted the archbishop, and with the situation becoming increasingly violent, Thomas made no attempt to hide from them in the dark recesses of the Cathedral but freely accepted death at their hands. When the terrified monks carried away his body, they found that he had worn a lice-ridden hairshirt next to his skin and had been daily whipped. We may be less inclined than contemporaries to take this as a mark of sanctity, but must at least admit that it indicates sincere penitence and stands in marked contrast to the outward pride of the archbishop.

What Becket achieved by his martyrdom remains a matter of debate. Certainly he reunited the English Church, which had been rent asunder by his uncompromising stand on matters of principle. The bitter enemies of his latter

RIGHT *Thomas embarks for England on 1st December 1170, as shown in* The Becket Leaves. *He is warned of treachery by Milo, chaplain of the Count of Boulogne.*

BELOW *News of the young king's coronation reaches Thomas (left) and the pope (right), as shown in* The Becket Leaves. *Becket was furious at this violation of the traditional right of Canterbury to crown English kings. The affront prompted him to return from exile, although none of the fundamental issues at stake had been resolved.*

...diunt ... viso ventos: occurrit Milo collector nauli nuncians insidias parari applicanti. Idem nuntiant advenientes.

Dunt li prodom le vout garnir
Atant regarde e voit venir
Milun, quide k'il ert desir
Fet demander, e fet venir
Sire, dist Miles, n'est pas si
Ke vieng pas fet demandé ci
Einz vus di un mandement
De part le cunte triste e dolent
Kel vus puis sanz les mes dire
Aturnez sunt pur vus ocire
De adversers grant assemblee
De la la mer cuntre vus arivee
Quant ad le mandement oi
Tut liez e baudz li respundi
Dengleterre sui ases pres
Seint sui si pur tant passer les
Droit est ke Canterebire
Des ore sun pastur desire
Set anz ad ke io ni fui
Ki du liu arceuesque fui
Itant regarde vers la rive
Vit k'une nef se arive
Hom demande quele est venue

Milun s'en vient ki ert siant
Au passageur de Withsant
Sire volez ke vous vus cunte
De part mun seignur le cunte
De Buloinne. Armee gent
De la mer par mi el vus atent
Si nuvele fust seue
Del arceuesque en Engletere
Cil dient ne volent tere
Kil disoient espessement
Kil vendroit novelement
Dunt grant ioie eurent e hait
Mais un de eus une part les trait
Ki dist: retraez vus chaitifs
Semble il vus lunges ke estes vifs
Des chevaliers une grant rute
De la vus atent sanz dute
Ki prez sunt e apareillez
De vus ocire quant vendrez
Mut est la terre esmeue
Cuntre vostre premere venue
La chesun tute si vus metent
Larceuesque e suens tut rettent

Par une nef ke est arivee
Est sa parole acertee
Vient cil k'arivez sunt
Gent armee mil de frunt
Gueite quant arriverez
Ke soiez tut tost detrenchez
Par larceuesque Roger
K'empreistes de curucer
E les evesques ke avez
Suspenduz e escumengez
Oue les evesques ki i sunt
Ki cuntre vus sunt tut de frunt
Renaud de Wareinne i est
Li visquens Gervese prest
E Randouf de Broc ki la
Li arceuesque escumenia
Od grant cumpaignie armee
Tut ensemble afiancee
Atendent sur la marine
Ki nuit e iur guetter ne fine
Ne serez plus tost arivez
Ke pris soiez e detrenchez. Cest esbaie.
Quant tute sa cumpaignie. Co ot. mut

De douz mals doit hom le meindre
Eslire. mieuz nus valt atendre
Ke destre hastifs e engres
Par quei repentirum apres
Larcevesqes lur respunt
He place a deu ki fist le mund
Ke io pur tant tel pour eie
Ke de mun purpos me retreie
Engleterre vei io de ci
Jo i enterrai. si sai de fi
A tur ne mest occisiun
De mort i suffrai passiun
Puis lan del incarnaciun
Cum nus en escrit lisum
Mil e cent. seissante e dis
De sun exil. setime meis uit
El secund iur u terz daduent
Se mist en mer priveement
Par nuit sariua a sandwic

Quant en engleterre arive
Muz i latendent a la rive
Pour lui ki sa beneiciun
Demandent par devociun
Mais reaus demandent pur quei
Suspent les prelaz lu rei
Cele part sunt alez tols
Quant la nef estoit venue
Par la croiz fu tost cunue
Li paisant grant ioie en unt
Ke tuit i acurru sunt
Cist esturcez e cest abat
En la mer entre lur prelat
Vunt pur li receivre a ioie
Dieu li enhaut kil oie
Benoit seit ki est venuz
El nun deu soit receuz
Atant es vus venent bruianz
Chevalers armez e serganz

years recognised the holiness of his end, and he became a model of episcopal resistance to government tyranny which was constantly cited to the eve of the Reformation. It is difficult to know what Henry II believed to be the outcome. The settlement which he reached with papal legates at Avranches in Normandy in May 1172 was a bargaining process rather than a royal capitulation. He agreed to abolish all evil customs which he had introduced but, since his entire case had been based on the situation in his grandfather's reign, he felt he had lost little. He did renounce jurisdiction over criminous clerks, but those forest offences which brought great profit to the crown were excluded from this exemption. Henry and his sons appointed the same sort of men to bishoprics after 1172 as before. Yet the king suffered public humiliation when, on 12th July 1174, he came on a pilgrimage to Canterbury and was flogged by the monks before the tomb. His reward came swiftly, for the very next day the English sector of the great rebellion of 1173–74, which was the greatest crisis of

LEFT *Thomas lands at Sandwich, from* The Becket Leaves. *The king's vassals, under the Sheriff of Kent, line the shore in hostile attitudes. Becket was protected from them by his old enemy John of Oxford, who had masterminded the king's campaign against him but now escorted him home.*

ABOVE *The death of Thomas Becket: this is the earliest known pictorial representation of Becket's martyrdom, in a manuscript dating to about 1180. It precedes a copy of the* Life of Becket *by John of Salisbury, the greatest English scholar of the 12th century and a friend of Becket's. On the left, Reginald FitzUrse among the knights strikes the first blow; on the right the four murderers do penance at the tomb.*

LEFT *This is a 15th-century version of the martyrdom (or rather a copy after the now faded original, a panel from Henry IV's tomb in north Trinity Chapel aisle). Becket is shown encircled by his persecutors, in a composition recalling that of Christ flagellated or crowned with thorns.*

BELOW *The Becket* Châsse. *This is one of many reliquary caskets showing Becket's martyrdom. It was made at Limoges in the 13th century. Limoges specialised in enamel work throughout the Middle Ages. Now in the Burrell Collection, it may originally have belonged to a Kentish town church and by the 18th century was in the collection of Horace Walpole at Strawberry Hill. On the side, it portrays the martyrdom with the Hand of God stretching down through a cloud. On the lid is St Thomas in apotheosis between two angels.*

his reign, collapsed and William the Lion, King of the Scots, was captured at Alnwick. Still, the penance demonstrated that, however much practical control English kings might still exercise over the Church in the realm, there were limits to the measures of coercion which they could employ.

Sixteen months before Henry did penance, in February 1173, Thomas had been canonised by Pope Alexander III. The murder had shocked western Christendom, and some thought that the pope had delayed unduly. At Canterbury the first miracle had occurred on the night of the martyrdom, and their multiplication eventually caused the hesitant monks in April 1171 to open to pilgrims the crypt where the archbishop had been buried. The hostility of royal officials to the burgeoning cult lessened once Henry himself was absolved of complicity in the murder.

Over 700 miracles are recorded in the decade after the assassination, and after Becket's canonisation the beneficiaries included persons from the upper echelons of

RIGHT *Martyrdom of Thomas Becket. This representation of Becket's martyrdom is one of several leaves inserted into a 13th-century English Psalter but which probably came from a 12th-century manuscript. The leader of the knights, Reginald FitzUrse, is distinguished by the heraldic device of a bear on his shield. The clerk whose arm is about to be severed by a sword-stroke is Edward Grim, who became one of Becket's biographers.*

LEFT *An embroidered depiction in silk of St Thomas Becket holding his primatial cross and a sword, the instrument of his martyrdom. This is one of a series of six saints associated with Canterbury from a clerical cope which was used by Canon John Shirley in the mid 20th century and is still in occasional use today.*

ABOVE *Stained glass in the Trinity Chapel. Pilgrims pray at the original low tomb in the eastern crypt, where St Thomas was buried from 1170 to 1220. The marble coffin was enclosed in a stone box with four port-holes, large enough for sick pilgrims to huddle as close as possible to the holy body.*

society and many from abroad, particularly France. By 1200 the cult, and ampoules containing the martyr's diluted blood, had spread all over western Europe, from Iceland, where a saga about the saint was composed, to Spain and Sicily. Canterbury became a great pilgrimage centre, the rival of Rome and Compostella, and it was almost a happy accident that a fire in 1174 necessitated the reconstruction of the entire east end of the Cathedral. This created a spectacular new shrine, although the body was not, in fact, translated from the crypt until 7 July 1220. The shrine was described by a Venetian visitor nearly three hundred years later:

Notwithstanding its great size, it is entirely covered with plates of pure gold. But the gold is scarcely visible beneath a profusion of gems, including sapphires, diamonds, rubies and emeralds. Everywhere that the eye turns something even more beautiful appears. The beauty of the materials is enhanced by the astonishing skill of human hands. Exquisite designs have been carved all over it and immense gems worked delicately into the patterns.

Far fewer miracles occurred at this magnificent shrine, however, than had at the simple sarcophagus in the crypt.

LEFT *King Henry II does penance at the tomb on 12 July 1174, as shown in 13th-century stained glass from Trinity Chapel in Canterbury Cathedral. At the height of the crisis of his reign, with simultaneous rebellion in all his territories fostered by his external enemies, Henry came on pilgrimage to Canterbury. He was ceremonially beaten by monks and bishops, made a large offering and lay in prayer all night. On the next day, his enemy the King of Scots was captured at Alnwick.*

BELOW *A sequence of twelve magnificent stained glass windows (the Miracle Windows) in the Trinity Chapel commemorates Becket's works and miracles. The early 13th-century panels shown here tell the story of the cure of the daughters of Godbald of Boxley. Both were born lame. One was cured after a vision in a dream and went to Canterbury to give thanks. The other complained at the unfairness of being left behind and she was also cured after a dream. The curing of lameness and the visionary nature of miraculous cures are recurrent themes in the Miracle Windows.*

RIGHT *Shrine of St Alban, St Alban's Cathedral. The shrine of St Alban was rebuilt in 1302-08 and restored in the 1990s, and gives some idea of how Becket's shrine would have appeared in its setting. The wooden gallery in the background was for custodians to watch over the shrine. There was also a watching chamber overlooking Becket's tomb.*

SANCTE ALBANE ORA PRO NOBIS
ALBANE ORA PRO NOBIS

It is probable that the cult of St Thomas was declining in popularity even before the end of the fourteenth century, when Chaucer's *The Canterbury Tales* told the stories of a diverse group of pilgrims on their way to Becket's shrine. Shifts in popular piety caused the cult to be eclipsed by sites with relics of Christ himself or His mother. Yet hordes of pilgrims still attended the jubilee, held every fifty years after the translation of 1220, or great occasions such as the Black Prince's funeral of 1376. The only attacks and slurs came from a few isolated Lollard heretics, one of whom was excommunicated as late as 1532 for insulting the martyr.

When the end came, it was with remarkable suddenness. In 1536, when the Reformation was well under way in England, the government turned against the 'papist' archbishop who had resisted royal domination of the English church in an earlier age. In September 1538 the shrine was demolished, the bones dispersed and St Thomas's treasure carted off to Westminster. All liturgical commemoration was banned and a royal proclamation announced Becket to have been a rebel and a traitor. A spurious trial was held to 'prove' these allegations. The zeal with which Henry VIII and his servants attempted to eradicate all memory of St Thomas of Canterbury, however, merely testifies to the example that he had provided for generations: that there is a law higher than the will of worldly princes, and that secular tyranny must, in God's name, be resisted even unto death.

◆ ◆ ◆

LEFT *Trinity Chapel vaulting, showing the boss over the shrine of St Thomas from which the pulley to raise the wooden cover of the tomb chest was suspended.*

THE TABARD

CANTER-
-BURY
LVI

PREVIOUS PAGE
Chaucer's Pilgrims, *by Eileen Thorne. In this recent painting, pilgrims are shown winding their way along the road that leads to Canterbury. As then, so today, the story of St Thomas has universal appeal to all classes of society, from the aristocracy to the lowest ranks of the afflicted.*

Picture Credits

Sonia Halliday and Laura Lushington: front cover, pp 2, 10/11, 31, 32/33, 34, 40
Cathedral Enterprises: back cover, 3, 27, 30, 38/39
The Wormsley Library: pp 1, 9, 15, 16/17, 18 *(below),* 20/21, 22, 23, 24/25
John McNeill: pp 4/5
*Canterbury Cathedral Archives: p.*6 *(top)*
*The National Archives, Kew: p.*6 *(below)*
*Trinity College, Cambridge: p.*7 *(MS R*17.1*)*
AKG: pp 12/13 *(Schütze/Rodemann),* 18 *(top),* 19 *(all Hervé Champollion)*
*Corbis: p.*14
*British Library. All rights reserved: p.*26 *(Cotton MS Claudius BII); p.*29 *(Harley MS* 5102*)*
*Culture and Sport Glasgow (Museums): p.*28
Angelo Hornak: pp 36/37
*Donato Cinicolo: p.*35

www.cathedral-enterprises.co.uk

Published by Cathedral Enterprises Ltd and Scala Publishers, Northburgh House, 10 *Northburgh Street, London EC1V 0AT*

This revised edition published 2009
Project management by Jessica Hodge
Designed by Guy Callaby
Printed in Turkey
ISBN 978-1-85759-622-9